DINOSAURS

IGUANODON

BY ANGELA LIM

An Imprint of Abdo Publishing
abdobooks.com

abdobooks.com

Published by Abdo Publishing, a division of ABDO, PO Box 398166, Minneapolis, Minnesota 55439.

Printed in the United States of America, North Mankato, Minnesota.
052025
092025

Cover Photo: Daniel Eskridge/Shutterstock Images
Interior Photos: Daniel Eskridge/Shutterstock Images, 4–5; Album/Florilegius/Science Source, 6; Alice Turner/Stocktrek Images/Getty Images, 9; The Natural History Museum, London/Science Source, 10, 16; Shutterstock Images, 12–13, 25; ZU_09/DigitalVision Vectors/Getty Images, 14; Roger Harris/Science Source, 17; Paul D. Stewart/Science Source, 18; Thierry Monasse/Getty Images News/Getty Images, 20–21; New York Public Library/Science Source, 22; Toho Company/Photofest, 26; Leonello Calvetti/Science Photo Library/Getty Images, 28–29

Editor: Kari Cornell
Series Designer: Mary Shaw

Library of Congress Control Number: 2024949007

Publisher's Cataloging-in-Publication Data

Names: Lim, Angela, author.
Title: Iguanodon / by Angela Lim
Description: Minneapolis, Minnesota: Abdo Publishing, 2026 | Series: Dinosaurs | Includes online resources and index.
Identifiers: ISBN 9781098297343 (lib. bdg.) | ISBN 9798384919865 (ebook)
Subjects: LCSH: Iguanodon--Juvenile literature. | Dinosaurs--Juvenile literature. | Herbivores--Juvenile literature. | Paleontology--Juvenile literature. | Extinct animals--Juvenile literature.
Classification: DDC 568.19--dc23

CONTENTS

Iguanodon ate fruits, flowering plants, ferns, and horsetail grass, an ancient plant that has grown on Earth for about 350 million years.

CHAPTER 1

ALL IN THE THUMBS

A **herd** of *Iguanodon* (ih-GWAH-nuh-dahn) roams near a river. The dinosaurs' powerful legs trample the grass. They drink water and use their beaks to pick and chew horsetail grass. This sturdy grass grows near water.

Some scientists think *Iguanodon* used its tail to balance on its two hind legs.

Ridged teeth line the backs of their mouths. These teeth grind tough plant material.

The *Iguanodon* herd comes across a fruit tree. One *Iguanodon* rears back on its hind legs. It steadies itself with its stiff tail. The dinosaur stretches out a **forelimb** to grab some fruit. Its thumb ends in a sharp spike. The *Iguanodon* uses its thumb to pierce the fruit. The spike removes the fruit's pit.

Suddenly, a *Torvosaurus* makes its way to the riverbank. It lets out a roar. The large **predator** lunges at the *Iguanodon*. The *Iguanodon* slashes at the other dinosaur with its thumb spikes. Deep gashes mark the chest of the *Torvosaurus*.

The *Iguanodon* has successfully defended itself. The predator flees. It will have to find a meal somewhere else.

Dinosaur Basics

Iguanodon and *Torvosaurus* are two examples of dinosaurs. Dinosaurs were large reptiles.

They first roamed the Earth about 250 million years ago. Dinosaurs are **extinct**. The last dinosaur died about 66 million years ago. The period of time when dinosaurs were alive is called the Mesozoic Era.

Today, **paleontologists** study dinosaur remains called fossils. These include dinosaur

What Happened to the Dinosaurs?

Several events likely caused dinosaurs to die off. A huge asteroid crashed into Earth. It sent clouds of dust into the sky. The dust blocked sunlight. This caused the **climate** to become much colder. Sea levels also began to rise. And a series of volcanic eruptions transformed Earth. These changes to the climate and the land made it impossible for dinosaurs to survive.

Iguanodon's jaw and skull bones had flexible joints to make it easier to chew tough plant material.

bones, teeth, and footprints. These remains help scientists learn about different dinosaurs. Some dinosaurs, such as *Iguanodon*, ate plants. Others ate animals. *Iguanodon* was a slow-moving dinosaur. But other dinosaurs could run quickly.

Iguanodon's thumb spikes, *top*, may have been used to strip leaves from trees and bushes.

Fossils provide a glimpse into the past. They reveal the animals and plants that lived long ago. Dinosaur fossils show how these animal species survived for millions of years. Studying fossils provides clues about how Earth's **climate** has changed. Scientists believe that climate change is one reason dinosaurs became extinct. Weather patterns still shift. Studying dinosaurs may help people learn more about how climate affects life today.

PRIMARY SOURCE

Mary H. Schweitzer is a paleontologist. She wrote about the importance of studying dinosaurs:

> [Studying fossils] helps us compare today's climate changes . . . with long-ago shifts before humans existed.

Source: Mary H. Schweitzer. "Dinosaurs Offer a Rich Field for Study of the Human Era." *Scientific American*, 1 June 2014, scientificamerican.com. Accessed 13 Aug. 2024.

Comparing Texts

Think about the quote. Does it support the information in this chapter? Or does it give a different perspective? Explain how in a few sentences.

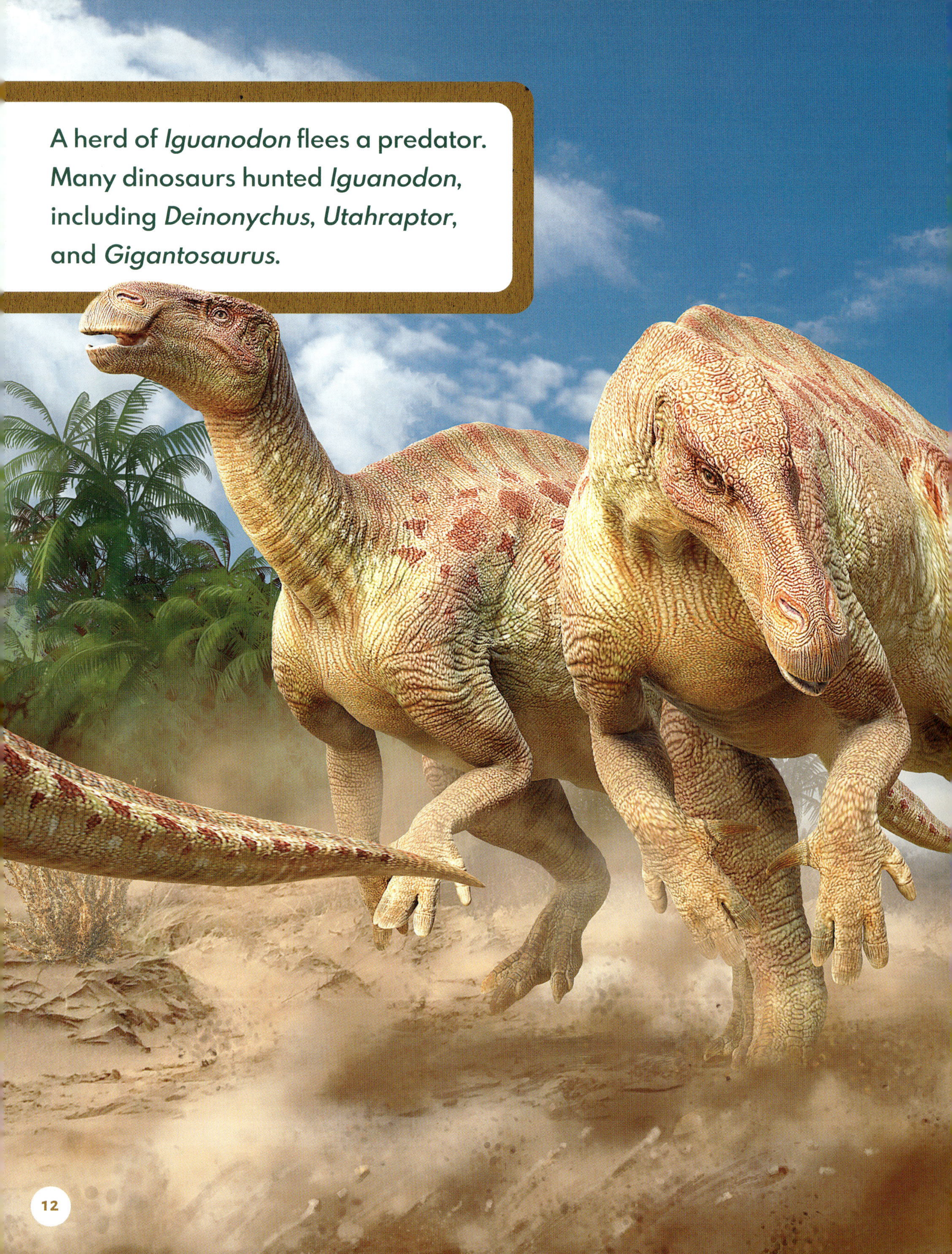

A herd of *Iguanodon* flees a predator. Many dinosaurs hunted *Iguanodon*, including *Deinonychus*, *Utahraptor*, and *Gigantosaurus*.

CHAPTER 2

IDENTIFYING *IGUANODON*

Iguanodon was a large dinosaur. It was 33 feet (10 m) tall. This is roughly the height of a three-story house. *Iguanodon* was also very heavy. It weighed around 4.4 tons (4 metric tons). This is a little heavier than a hippopotamus.

Iguanodon used its sharp thumb spike to defend itself against predators and to grab food.

Iguanodon bones show that the dinosaur had five fingers on its front limbs. Both thumbs ended with a large spike. The spike may have been used for protection. Some scientists think that *Iguanodon* used its thumbs against predators. It may have also used the spike on its thumb to strip leaves from plants. The thumb spikes could break apart seeds as well.

Remains of *Iguanodon* teeth show that they were ridged. The teeth were similar in shape to the teeth of modern-day iguanas. The name *Iguanodon* means "iguana tooth."

Eating Habits

Paleontologists have studied the skull of *Iguanodon*. The skull's shape shows that the dinosaur had a beak. It also likely had a long tongue. The tongue helped *Iguanodon* move food around in its mouth. *Iguanodon* may have used its tongue to grab leaves as well.

This tooth was the first *Iguanodon* tooth discovered.

Iguanodon Behavior

Iguanodon lived near rivers and streams. Ferns and horsetail grew near these water sources.

Iguanodon usually grazed on all four legs, but it may have reared up on its hind legs to reach for leaves or fruits.

These plants made up a large part of the dinosaur's diet.

Iguanodon walked on four legs. It may have been able to stand on its hind legs. This would help it reach leaves on high branches.

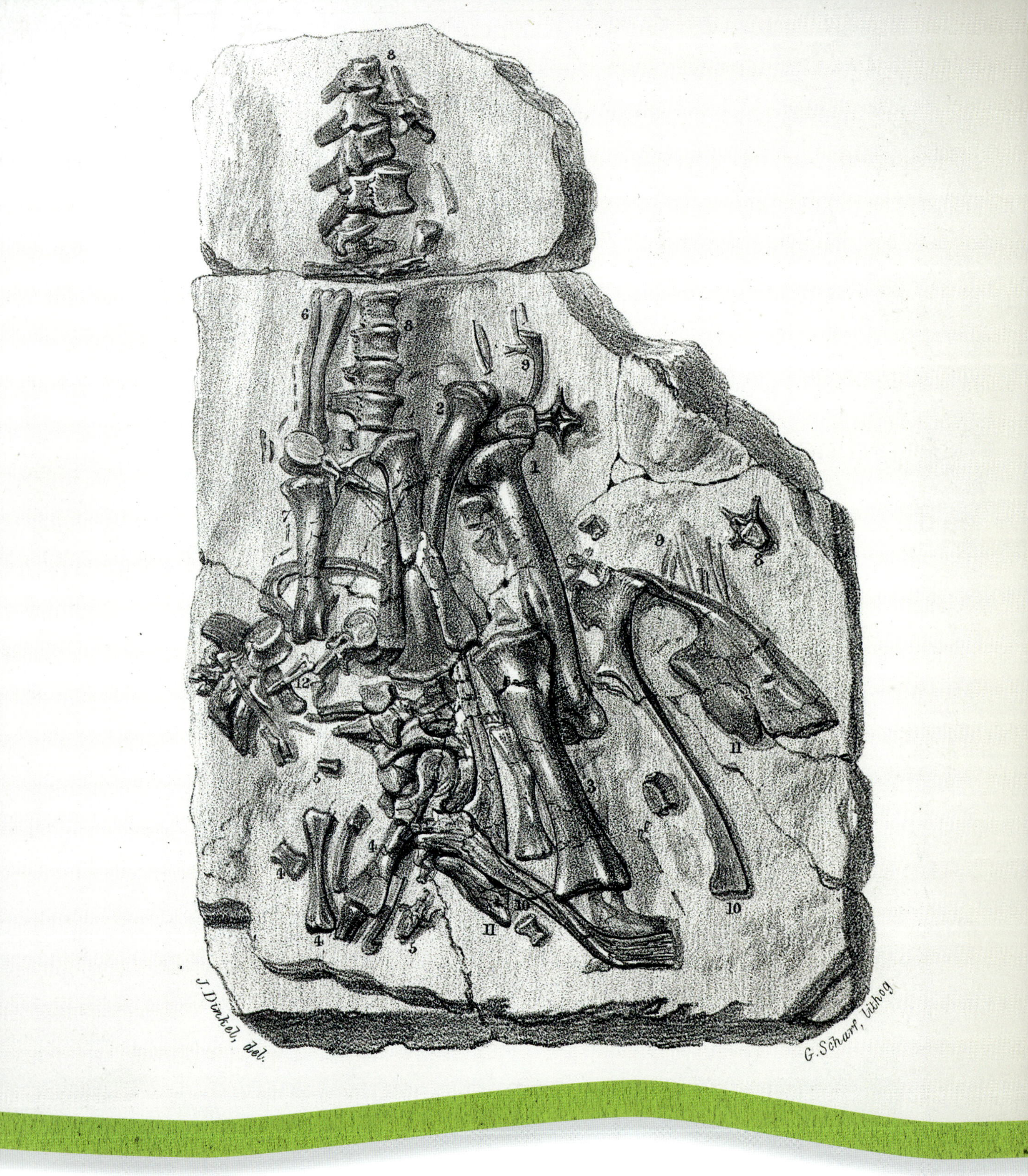

The first *Iguanodon* skeleton was discovered in a quarry in Maidstone, Kent, United Kingdom.

But paleontologists disagree on whether *Iguanodon* could actually stand on two legs.

Paleontologists have found multiple *Iguanodon* fossils close together. This means the dinosaurs probably traveled in herds. Traveling in a big group made it more difficult for predators to attack.

Explore Online

Visit the website below. Does it give any new information about *Iguanodon* that wasn't in Chapter Two?

Iguanodon

abdocorelibrary.com/iguanodon

The *Iguanodon* skeleton displayed at the Royal Belgium Institute of Natural Sciences weighs more than 4.4 tons (4 metric tons).

CHAPTER 3

IGUANODON DISCOVERIES

Iguanodon was the second dinosaur species to be discovered. It helped scientists learn about dinosaurs. *Iguanodon* was first discovered in 1822 in the United Kingdom. Mary Ann Mantell found teeth stuck in a rock.

Belgian paleontologist Louis Antoine Marie Joseph Dollo worked with a team to assemble *Iguanodon* skeletons found in a Belgian mine.

Her husband, Dr. Gideon Mantell, studied the set of *Iguanodon* teeth.

Dr. Mantell compared the teeth to those of living reptiles. He found out that the teeth were like a bigger version of iguana teeth.

The teeth were early **evidence** that dinosaurs were reptiles.

Other early paleontologists also looked at the teeth. Around 1824, Georges Cuvier suggested the teeth may have belonged to a plant-eating reptile. Cuvier is sometimes considered the father of paleontology.

Dinosaur Studies

Dinosaurs were not studied until the 1800s. In fact, the word *dinosaur* was not invented until 1842. It combined two ancient Greek words. *Deinos* is the ancient Greek word for "fearfully great." *Sauros* is ancient Greek for "lizard." Today, there are more than 700 known dinosaur species.

Later, *Iguanodon* bones were discovered. The first reconstructions of *Iguanodon* skeletons were not correct. Paleontologists thought the dinosaur's thumb spike was a horn. They placed it on *Iguanodon*'s snout. Then in 1878, miners discovered fossils in a mine in Belgium. There were nearly 30 complete *Iguanodon* skeletons.

From these skeletons, paleontologists learned that the spike was part of *Iguanodon*'s thumb. But they displayed the skeletons standing on their two hind legs. Now scientists think that *Iguanodon* mostly walked on all fours.

Iguanodon in Pop Culture

Iguanodon is a popular dinosaur in media. It appeared in the 2000 Disney film *Dinosaur.*

How a Fossil Forms

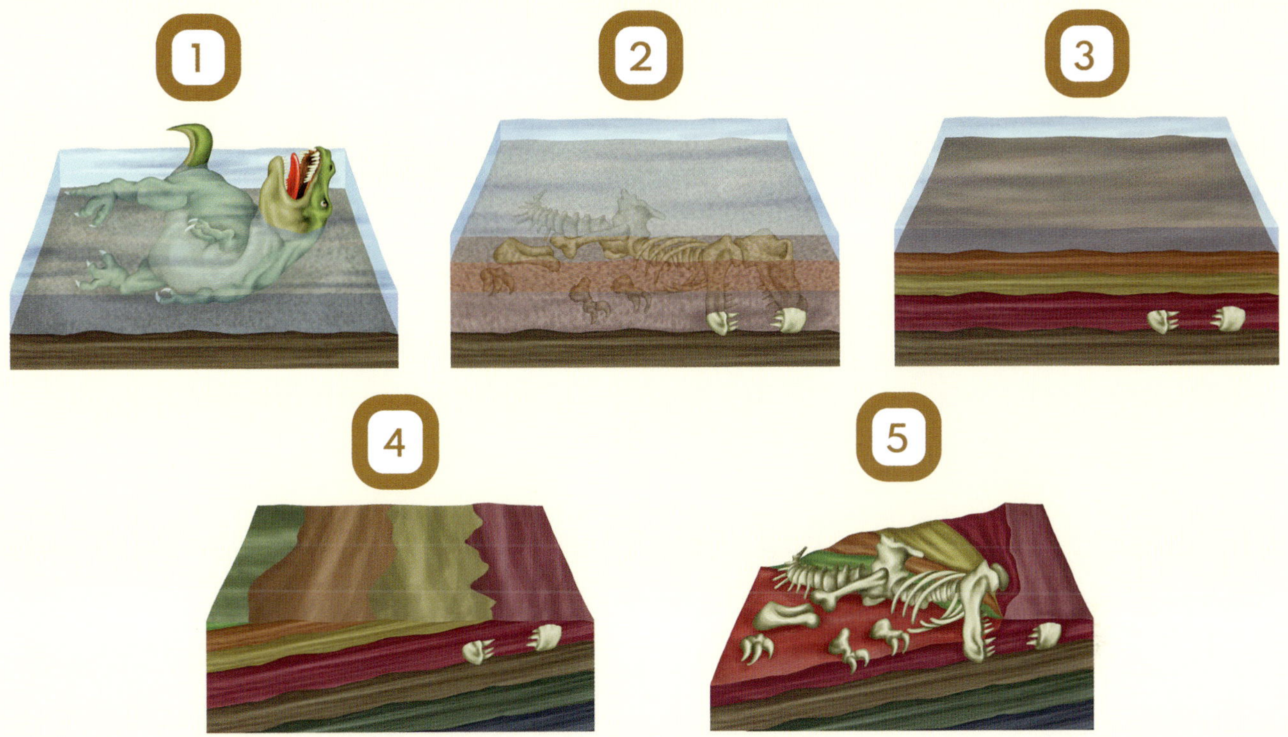

1. A dinosaur dies.
2. The soft parts of its body decay. The hard parts remain. This includes bones and teeth.
3. Layers of dirt cover the dinosaur's body.
4. Minerals from the earth seep into the dinosaur bones. This turns the bones into rocks.
5. Earth's landmasses move gradually. This can cause fossils to come closer to the surface.

Conditions have to be just right for bones to become fossils. The process takes thousands of years.

Iguanodon was an inspiration for Godzilla. This monster terrorizes an island off the coast of Japan in *Godzilla 1985*.

It is also one of the dinosaurs that inspired the making of *Godzilla*. The movie monster made its first appearance in 1954. Godzilla has a head and body that are similar to those of an *Iguanodon*.

Unlike *Iguanodon*, Godzilla moves on two legs. *Tyrannosaurus rex* walked on its hind legs. It also served as a model for Godzilla. *Stegosaurus* was an inspiration too. Both the dinosaur and Godzilla have bony plates along their backs.

Iguanodon has helped shape how dinosaurs appear in pop culture. It also was a major discovery in paleontology. It took years to construct *Iguanodon*'s skeleton correctly. But scientists have learned a lot from these dinosaurs.

Further Evidence

Look at the website below. Does it give any new evidence to support Chapter Three?

How Are Fossils Made?

abdocorelibrary.com/iguanodon

DINO DETAILS

Sharp beak with iguana-like teeth to eat plants

Powerful thumb spikes to defend against predators

Long, muscular tail that may have been used for balance
Primarily walked on four legs to support its weight

Glossary

climate
average weather conditions in an area over a long period of time

evidence
information that supports an idea

extinct
no longer exists

forelimb
a front limb such as an arm or wing

herd
a group of animals who travel together

paleontologist
a scientist who studies fossils

predator
an animal that hunts other animals

Online Resources

To learn more about *Iguanodon* and late-Mesozoic dinosaurs, visit our free resource websites below.

Visit **abdocorelibrary.com** or scan this QR code for free Common Core resources for teachers and students, including vetted activities, multimedia, and booklinks, for deeper subject comprehension.

Visit **abdobooklinks.com** or scan this QR code for free additional online weblinks for further learning. These links are routinely monitored and updated to provide the most current information available.

Learn More

Giedd, Steph. *Triceratops.* Abdo, 2024.

Hulick, Kathryn. *Dinosaurs.* Abdo, 2023.

Rubin, Sean. *The Iguanodon's Horn.* Clarion, 2024.

Index

About the Author

Angela Lim is an MFA student in poetry at Indiana University. *Stegosaurus* is her favorite dinosaur.